FI

by Iain Gray

LangSyne
PUBLISHING
WRITING *to* REMEMBER

LangSyne
PUBLISHING
WRITING *to* REMEMBER

79 Main Street, Newtongrange,
Midlothian EH22 4NA
Tel: 0131 344 0414
E-mail: info@lang-syne.co.uk
www.langsyneshop.co.uk

Design by Dorothy Meikle
Printed by Printwell Ltd

ISBN 978-1-85217-256-5

Flynn

MOTTO:

Not without danger
(and) Honour is the reward of virtue.

CREST:

A hand grasping a serpent.

NAME variations include:

Ó Floinn *(Gaelic)*
O'Flynn
Flinn
O'Lynn
Lynn

Chapter one:
Origins of Irish surnames

According to an old saying, there are two types of Irish – those who actually are Irish and those who wish they were.

This sentiment is only one example of the allure that the high romance and drama of the proud nation's history holds for thousands of people scattered across the world today.

It's a sad fact, however, that the vast majority of Irish surnames are found far beyond Irish shores, rather than on the Emerald Isle itself.

The population stood at around eight million souls in 1841, but today it stands at fewer than six million.

This is mainly a tragic consequence of the potato famine, also known as the Great Hunger, which devastated Ireland between 1845 and 1849.

The Irish peasantry had become almost wholly reliant for basic sustenance on the potato, first introduced from the Americas in the seventeenth century.

When the crop was hit by a blight, at least 800,000 people starved to death while an estimated two million others were forced to seek a new life far from their native shores – particularly in America, Canada, and Australia.

The effects of the potato blight continued until about 1851, by which time a firm pattern of emigration had become established.

Ireland's loss, however, was to the gain of the countries in which the immigrants settled, contributing enormously, as their descendants do today, to the well being of the nations in which their forefathers settled.

But those who were forced through dire circumstance to establish a new life in foreign parts never forgot their roots, or the proud heritage and traditions of the land that gave them birth.

Nor do their descendants.

It is a heritage that is inextricably bound up in the colourful variety of Irish names themselves – and the origin and history of these names forms an integral part of the vibrant drama that is the nation's history, one of both glorious fortune and tragic misfortune.

This history is well documented, and one of the most important and fascinating of the earliest sources are *The Annals of the Four Masters*, compiled between 1632 and 1636 by four friars at the Franciscan Monastery in County Donegal.

Compiled from earlier sources, and purporting to go back to the Biblical Deluge, much of the material takes in the mythological origins and history of Ireland and the Irish.

This includes tales of successive waves of invaders and settlers such as the Fomorians, the Partholonians, the Nemedians, the Fir Bolgs, the Tuatha De Danann, and the Laigain.

Of particular interest are the *Milesian Genealogies*, because the majority of Irish clans today claim a descent from either Heremon, Ir, or Heber – three of the sons of Milesius, a king of what is now modern day Spain.

These sons invaded Ireland in the second millennium B.C, apparently in fulfilment of a mysterious prophecy received by their father.

This Milesian lineage is said to have ruled Ireland for nearly 3,000 years, until the island came under the sway of England's King Henry II in 1171 following what is known as the Cambro-Norman invasion.

This is an important date not only in Irish history in general, but for the effect the invasion subsequently had for Irish surnames.

'Cambro' comes from the Welsh, and 'Cambro-Norman' describes those Welsh knights of Norman origin who invaded Ireland.

But they were invaders who stayed, inter-marrying with the native Irish population and founding their own proud dynasties that bore Cambro-Norman names such as Archer, Barbour, Brannagh, Fitzgerald, Fitzgibbon, Fleming, Joyce, Plunkett, and Walsh – to name only a few.

These 'Cambro-Norman' surnames that still flourish throughout the world today form one of the three main categories in which Irish names can be placed – those of Gaelic-Irish, Cambro-Norman, and Anglo-Irish.

Previous to the Cambro-Norman invasion of the twelfth century, and throughout the earlier invasions and settlement of those wild bands of sea rovers known as the Vikings in the eighth and ninth centuries, the population of the island was relatively small, and it was normal for a person to be identified through the use of only a forename.

But as population gradually increased and there were many more people with the same forename, surnames were adopted to distinguish one person, or one community, from another.

Individuals identified themselves with their own particular tribe, or 'tuath', and this tribe – that also became known as a clann, or clan – took its name from some distinguished ancestor who had founded the clan.

The Gaelic-Irish form of the name Kelly, for example, is Ó Ceallaigh, or O'Kelly, indicating descent from an original 'Ceallaigh', with the 'O' denoting 'grandson of.' The name was later anglicised to Kelly.

The prefix 'Mac' or 'Mc', meanwhile, as with the clans of the Scottish Highlands, denotes 'son of.'

Although the Irish clans had much in common with their Scottish counterparts, one important difference lies in what are known as 'septs', or branches, of the clan.

Septs of Scottish clans were groups who often bore an entirely different name from the clan name but were under the clan's protection.

In Ireland, septs were groups that shared the same name and who could be found scattered throughout the four provinces of Ulster, Leinster, Munster, and Connacht.

The 'golden age' of the Gaelic-Irish clans, infused as

their veins were with the blood of Celts, pre-dates the Viking invasions of the eighth and ninth centuries and the Norman invasion of the twelfth century, and the sacred heart of the country was the Hill of Tara, near the River Boyne, in County Meath.

Known in Gaelic as 'Teamhar na Rí', or Hill of Kings, it was the royal seat of the 'Ard Rí Éireann', or High King of Ireland, to whom the petty kings, or chieftains, from the island's provinces were ultimately subordinate.

It was on the Hill of Tara, beside a stone pillar known as the Irish 'Lia Fáil', or Stone of Destiny, that the High Kings were inaugurated and, according to legend, this stone would emit a piercing screech that could be heard all over Ireland when touched by the hand of the rightful king.

The Hill of Tara is today one of the island's main tourist attractions.

Opposition to English rule over Ireland, established in the wake of the Cambro-Norman invasion, broke out frequently and the harsh solution adopted by the powerful forces of the Crown was to forcibly evict the native Irish from their lands.

These lands were then granted to Protestant colonists, or 'planters', from Britain.

Many of these colonists, ironically, came from Scotland and were the descendants of the original 'Scotti', or 'Scots', who gave their name to Scotland after migrating there in the fifth century A.D., from the north of Ireland.

Colonisation entailed harsh penal laws being imposed on the majority of the native Irish population, stripping them practically of all of their rights.

The Crown's main bastion in Ireland was Dublin and its environs, known as the Pale, and it was the dispossessed peasantry who lived outside this Pale, desperately striving to eke out a meagre living.

It was this that gave rise to the modern-day expression of someone or something being 'beyond the pale'.

Attempts were made to stamp out all aspects of the ancient Gaelic-Irish culture, to the extent that even to bear a Gaelic-Irish name was to invite discrimination.

This is why many Gaelic-Irish names were anglicised with, for example, and noted above, Ó Ceallaigh, or O'Kelly, being anglicised to Kelly.

Succeeding centuries have seen strong revivals of Gaelic-Irish consciousness, however, and this has led to many families reverting back to the original form of their name, while the language itself is frequently found on the fluent tongues of an estimated 90,000 to 145,000 of the island's population.

Ireland's turbulent history of religious and political strife is one that lasted well into the twentieth century, a landmark century that saw the partition of the island into the twenty-six counties of the independent Republic of Ireland, or Eire, and the six counties of Northern Ireland, or Ulster.

Dublin, originally founded by Vikings, is now a vibrant

and truly cosmopolitan city while the proud city of Belfast is one of the jewels in the crown of Ulster.

It was Saint Patrick who first brought the light of Christianity to Ireland in the fifth century A.D.

Interpretations of this Christian message have varied over the centuries, often leading to bitter sectarian conflict – but the many intricately sculpted Celtic Crosses found all over the island are symbolic of a unity that crosses the sectarian divide.

It is an image that fuses the 'old gods' of the Celts with Christianity.

All the signs from the early years of this new millennium indicate that sectarian strife may soon become a thing of the past – with the Irish and their many kinsfolk across the world, be they Protestant or Catholic, finding common purpose in the rich tapestry of their shared heritage.

Meanwhile, many Irish clans and families proudly boast the heraldic device known as a Coat of Arms, as featured on our front cover.

The central motif of the Coat of Arms would originally have been what was borne on the shield of a warrior to distinguish himself from others on the battlefield.

Not featured on the Coat of Arms, but highlighted on page three, is the family motto and related crest – with the latter frequently different from the central motif.

Chapter two:

High kings and warriors

'Not without danger' is one of the mottos of the proud clan of Flynn, and it was certainly not without danger that they held sway for centuries throughout Ireland's provinces.

Although there were separate and unrelated septs of Flynns, what they all had in common was that their name derived from the Gaelic Ó Floinn, itself derived from 'flann', indicating reddish, or ruddy.

The western province of Connacht, in the area of present day Co. Roscommon, was home to one sept of Flynns while the southern province of Munster, in the area of present day Co. Cork was home to another sept.

Flynns were also to be found in the northern province of Ulster, mainly in the area of present day Co. Antrim.

In common with other native Irish clans, the Flynns trace a descent from Milesius, a king of what is now modern day Spain, and who had planned to invade Ireland in fulfilment of a mysterious Druidic prophecy.

Milesius died before he could launch his invasion across the sea to Ireland, but eight sons who included Amergin, Hebor, Ir, and Heremon undertook the task.

Five sons, including Ir, were killed in battle

against the Tuatha De Danann shortly after battling their way onto Irish soil.

This was soil, however, that Ir's offspring and the offspring of his brothers Heber and Heremon were destined to hold for centuries as warrior kings.

According to the Milesian genealogies, Heremon and Heber began to rule the land they had conquered from about 1699 B.C.

The Flynns of Ulster and Connacht claim a descent from Heremon, while those of Munster claim a descent from Ithe, an uncle of Milesius.

The Ulster Flynns originated in Connacht and that is why both septs were recognised as members of the tribal grouping known as the Dal Cuinn, or race of Cuinn, or Conn.

This was the legendary warrior king Conn Céthchathach, the Gaelic form for Conn of the Hundred Battles.

Ard Rí, or High King of Ireland from about 177 to 212 A.D. this progenitor, or ancestor, of the Flynns of today, figures prominently in what are known as the Fenian Cycle of tales, also known as the Ossianic Cycle and thought to date from the third century.

One of Conn's illustrious ancestors is said to have been no less than Goidel Glas, who is reputed to have created the Gaelic-Irish language after he combined and refined the 72 known languages of his time.

The result is the language of poets that runs throughout the Fenian Cycle.

As a youth, Conn is said to have met two mysterious figures who predicted he and his descendants would rule Ireland.

The strange figures who are reputed by legend to have appeared to Conn, enshrouded in mist, were a beautiful young maiden known as Sovranty – wearing a golden crown and seated on a crystal chair, she was accompanied by the sun god Lugh, patron of arts and crafts.

It is said they prophesied his descendants would rule until the death of the old Gods – which in fact did occur in the form of St. Patrick and the new religious pantheon of Christianity.

Conn attained the High Kingship after overthrowing Cathair Mór, also known as Mal, who had killed his father.

But his kingship was never secure because he had to fight a relentless succession of battles with his great rival Eogan Mór, also known as Mug Nadhat, king of the Dál nAraide, or Cruithe, who occupied the northeastern territories of Ireland.

It was because of the number of battles Conn fought with these Cruithne, or Picts, that he earned the title of Conn Céthchathach – Conn of the Hundred Battles.

The two rival kings achieved a temporary accommodation after the island was divided between themselves, the division starting at a ridge known as Eiscir Riada, which traverses the island from Galway Bay to Dublin.

Mug's territory in the south was known as Leth Moga Nuadht, while Conn's northern territory was known as Leth Cuinn.

But it was not long before the ambitious and fiercely proud pair were at each other's throats again.

Mug gained the upper hand for a time after storing up grain in his territories after taking heed of a dire Druidic prophecy of famine – but Conn eventually defeated his rival after taking him by cunning surprise in a night raid near present-day Tullamore, in County Offaly.

Conn consolidated his kingship over Ireland, but his success was short-lived, destined to die under the glinting blades of fifty warriors who had managed to breach the defences of his royal bastion of Tara after disguising themselves as women.

At the head of these warriors was the vengeful Tibride Tirech, son of the Cathair Mór whom Conn had killed years earlier in revenge for the death of his own father.

The Ulster Flynns also claim a descent from Carrell, or Colla Uais, one of the famed brothers known as the Three Collas, who carved out the kingdom of Airghialla, or Oriel, in Ulster.

To find how the three – Carrell, Muredach, and Aedh – came to acquire the designation of 'rebel' we have to go back through the dim mists of time to about 322 A.D. when the Ard Rí of Ireland was Fiachaidh Sraibtine.

He was their uncle, brother of their father Eocaidh

Dublein; adding to the lustre of the royal pedigree of the Collas was that their mother was a daughter of the King of Alba – as the kingdom of Scotland was then known.

Fiercely ambitious, the three brothers were not content simply to rest on the laurels of their impressive royal connections.

They yearned for the kingship of Ireland itself, but obstacles stood in their way in the persons of not only the Ard Rí himself but also his son and heir, Muredach Tirech.

Muredach won a decisive battle in Munster and, about to succeed his aging and ailing father to the throne, the Collas decided to take pre-emptive action.

Rallying their supporters they rebelled and defeated the king in battle and Carrell, or Colla Uais, took the throne.

Before the battle, the elderly king had been reminded by his Druid of an ancient curse that warned if he killed his three nephews then the fruits of his own loins would lose the sovereignty of Ireland forever.

More concerned with his posterity than with himself, the king appears to have only rather half-heartedly engaged in battle with the brothers – stoically prepared to die in the knowledge that some day the throne would revert back to his own progeny.

Colla Uais had been on the throne for four years when the former king's son, Muredach Tirech, managed to rally enough support to overthrow him and the Three Collas were driven from Ireland and into exile in Scotland.

They returned to Ireland three years later, perhaps confident that Muredach Tirech, aware of the ancient curse concerning the loss of the kingship to his own progeny should he kill the brothers, would not seek retribution for the death of his father.

Although he did not exactly embrace them with open arms, an accommodation was reached.

Later, no doubt hoping to see the back of his troublesome cousins, Muredach Tirech put forward the suggestion that they should kill two birds with one stone by waging war on the rival Ulaid of Ulster and taking their territory for their own.

The brothers agreed with alacrity and, after assembling a mighty army with the help of the king, they marched north into Ulster and defeated Fergus Fogha, king of the Ulaid, in a battle in 332 A.D. on the plain of Farney, in present day Co. Monaghan – but one of the brothers, Aedh, also known as Colla Menn, was killed.

The two remaining brothers now laid the foundations of what would become the Ulster kingdom of Airghialla, or Oriel.

What would become the sept of the Flynns of Ulster had formed part of the original invasion force of the province, and they trace a descent from Fiachra Tort, a son of Colla Uais.

Chapter three:

Wars of independence

What would ultimately prove to be the death knell of the ancient way of life of proud native Irish clans such as the Flynns was sounded in the late twelfth century Cambro-Norman invasion of the island, followed up and consolidated under Anglo-Norman invasion.

Twelfth century Ireland was far from being a unified nation, split up as it was into territories ruled over by squabbling chieftains such as Dermot MacMurrough, who ruled as kings in their own right – and this inter-clan rivalry worked to the advantage of the invaders.

In a series of bloody conflicts one chieftain, or king, would occasionally gain the upper hand over his rivals, and by 1156 the most powerful was Muirchertach MacLochlainn, king of the powerful O'Neills.

He was opposed by the equally powerful Rory O'Connor, king of the province of Connacht, but he increased his power and influence by allying himself with Dermot MacMurrough, king of Leinster.

MacLochlainn and MacMurrough were aware that the main key to the kingdom of Ireland was the thriving trading port of Dublin that had been established by invading Vikings, or Ostmen, in 852 A.D.

Dublin was taken by the combined forces of the Leinster

and Connacht kings, but when MacLochlainn died the Dubliners rose up in revolt and overthrew the unpopular MacMurrough.

A triumphant Rory O'Connor entered Dublin and was later inaugurated as Ard Rí, but MacMurrough was not one to humbly accept defeat.

He appealed for help from England's Henry II in unseating O'Connor, an act that was to radically affect the future course of Ireland's fortunes.

The English monarch agreed to help MacMurrough, but distanced himself from direct action by delegating his Norman subjects in Wales with the task.

These ambitious and battle-hardened barons and knights had first settled in Wales following the Norman Conquest of England in 1066 and, with an eye on rich booty, plunder, and lands, were only too eager to obey their sovereign's wishes and furnish MacMurrough with aid.

MacMurrough crossed the Irish Sea to Bristol, where he rallied powerful barons such as Robert Fitzstephen and Maurice Fitzgerald to his cause, along with Gilbert de Clare, Earl of Pembroke, and also known as Strongbow.

The mighty Norman war machine soon moved into action, and so fierce and disciplined was their onslaught on the forces of Rory O'Connor and his allies that by 1171 they had re-captured Dublin, in the name of MacMurrough, and other strategically important territories.

A nervous Henry II began to take cold feet over the

venture, realising that he may have created a rival in the form of a separate Norman kingdom in Ireland.

Accordingly, he landed on the island, near Waterford, at the head of a large army in October of 1171 with the aim of curbing the power of his Cambro-Norman barons.

Protracted war between the king and his barons was averted, however, when the barons submitted to the royal will, promising homage and allegiance in return for holding the territories they had conquered in the king's name.

Henry also received the submission and homage of many of the Irish chieftains, but much of Ulster remained a virtual 'no go' area for the Normans, with proud clans such as the Flynns determined to resist the invader.

One hero in this war of freedom and independence was Cumee O'Flynn, chieftain of the O'Flynns of what is now present day Co. Antrim.

Land that had for centuries been the territories of native Irish clans had been apportioned out by the English monarch to his powerful Norman barons, but many young and ambitious Norman knights were also determined to lay claim to territory.

Among them was Sir John DeCourcy, the youngest son of a knight from Somerset.

Assembling a force of about 300 other young knights and some mercenary Irish warriors, DeCourcy set off northwards from Dublin in the early weeks of 1177 with the aim of subjugating the northeastern Ulster kingdom of Ulidia.

He would ultimately prove successful, but not before facing particularly ferocious and determined opposition from the forces of Cumee O'Flynn, Rory MacDonlevy, king of the Ulidia, and other Ulster chieftains.

It was a brutal campaign.

By the beginning of February DeCourcy and his blood-crazed band of knights and warriors had taken Downpatrick – at terrible cost to the civilian population, with women and children indiscriminately slaughtered in the streets.

But DeCourcy's further progress northwards was hampered at every turn by the forces of Cumee O'Flynn and other chieftains, who waged brutal guerrilla warfare.

In one encounter in a mountain pass DeCourcy only narrowly managed to escape after a surprise assault was mounted on him by the bold O'Flynn.

A pitched battle between the two sides was eventually fought on June 24, 1177 – a bloody encounter that ended in defeat for O'Flynn and his fellow native Irish.

Bloodied but unbowed, however, the Irish continued their campaign of guerrilla warfare, and it was in one engagement that Cumee O'Flynn was killed.

DeCourcy managed to consolidate his conquest of Ulster but, ironically, was destined to die in prison in 1219 after his over reaching ambition led to him falling foul of the English Crown.

Over the succeeding centuries the Flynns would continue their opposition to the Crown.

An indication of the root of their resentment towards the Crown can be found in a desperate plea sent to Pope John XII by Roderick O'Carroll of Ely, Donald O'Neil of Ulster, and a number of other Irish chieftains, such as those of the Flynns, in 1318.

They stated: 'As it very constantly happens, whenever an Englishman, by perfidy or craft, kills an Irishman, however noble, or however innocent, be he clergy or layman, there is no penalty or correction enforced against the person who may be guilty of such wicked murder.

'But rather the more eminent the person killed and the higher rank which he holds among his own people, so much more is the murderer honoured and rewarded by the English, and not merely by the people at large, but also by the religious and bishops of the English race.'

The straw that finally broke the camel's back in relation to the uneasy relationship between the English Crown and the Flynns, in common with many other prominent Catholic Irish families, proved to be the policy of 'plantation', or settlement of loyal Protestants on land held by native Irish.

This started during the reign from 1491 to 1547 of Henry VIII, whose Reformation effectively outlawed the established Roman Catholic faith throughout his dominions.

This plantation continued throughout the subsequent reigns of Elizabeth I, James I (James VI of Scotland), and in the wake of the devastating Cromwellian invasion of 1649.

A number of Irish earls rebelled against the policy of

plantation and harsh penal policies against Catholics but, following their defeat at the battle of Kinsale in 1601 and the final suppression of the rebellion three years later in Ulster, their future existence hung by a precarious thread.

Three years later, in September of 1607 and in what is known as The Flight of the Earls, Hugh O'Neill, 2nd Earl of Tyrone and Rory O'Donnell, 1st Earl of Tyrconnel, sailed into foreign exile from the village of Rathmullan, on the shore of Lough Swilly, in Co. Donegal, accompanied by ninety loyal followers.

To many, this represented one of the final nails in the coffin of the ancient Gaelic order of ancient Irish clans such as the Flynns.

Further reeling blows to the Gaelic order were dealt in the wake of the Cromwellian invasion of 1649 and a policy of further plantation, while the order was doomed forever following the 'Glorious Revolution' of 1688 that brought the Protestant William of Orange and his wife Mary to the throne.

But a restoration of sorts of the fortunes of families such as the Flynns would later be found on foreign shores –where many would flourish, and still flourish to this day, in a diverse range of pursuits.

Chapter four:

On the world stage

One of the most flamboyant bearers of the name of Flynn was *Errol Flynn*, the Hollywood film star who was born in Hobart, Tasmania, in 1909.

Numerous scandals surrounded his later life, but his family background was ultra-respectable with his father, **Theodore Flynn**, a noted biologist who later in his career held the chair of zoology at Queen's University, in Belfast.

Errol Flynn proved to be rather a handful for his family from an early age – moving to Sydney, Australia, as a child he was later expelled from no less than two schools because of his non-conformist behaviour.

With the aid of financial backing from his exasperated parents the future film star moved as a young man to New Guinea, where he bought a tobacco plantation.

The venture proved a spectacular failure, as did a copper mining venture.

By 1933 he was back in Australia, where his matinee-idol looks won him a starring role in the film *In the Wake of the Bounty*.

It was then off to Britain, where he worked for a time with the Northampton Repertory Company – and it was while treading the boards with this small company that he was talent-spotted by an executive from the Warner Brothers film company and immediately signed up and whisked off to Hollywood as a contract actor.

He became an overnight success, winning the hearts of thousands of female fans worldwide as the swashbuckling star of films such as the 1935 *Captain Blood*, *The Adventurers of Robin Hood* and *The Dawn Patrol*, both from 1938, and the 1948 *Adventurers of Don Juan*.

His antics off camera became as famous as his antics on camera, as Flynn indulged in a veritable orgy of drinks, drugs, and womanising.

This came to a head in 1943 when, in a sensational trial, he was accused of the statutory rape of two teenage girls.

He was cleared off the charges and went on to star in more films including what would prove to be his last – the 1959 *Cuban Rebel Girls*.

It was after making this movie that during a trip to Canada along with young actress Beverly Aadland, whom it is thought he had planned to make his fourth wife, that he died of a heart attack.

Through his first marriage, to the actress Lili Damita, Flynn had a son, **Sean Flynn**, born in 1941.

He had a brief acting career, appearing in the 1964 *The Son of Captain Blood*, before turning to photo journalism.

On assignment in Cambodia in April of 1970 he and a fellow journalist disappeared, never to be seen again.

Believed to have been captured by factions of the

Vietcong and Khmer Rouge, both men were finally legally declared dead in 1984.

Also in the world of journalism, **John T. Flynn**, born in Bladensburg, Maryland, in 1882 and who died in 1964, was the American journalist and highly influential political commentator who was also one of the founders of the America First Committee

Errol Flynn is meanwhile believed to be the inspiration for the saying **'In Like Flynn'**, defined as being 'quickly and emphatically successful, usually in a sexual or romantic context.'

However another theory is that the saying stems from the career of the highly successful American political organiser **Edward J. Flynn**, a campaign manager for the Democratic Party during the 1930s and 1940s.

Born in 1960 in Waukegan, Illinois, **Neil Flynn** is the versatile American actor who is probably best known for his role as the janitor in the television series *Scrubs*, while **Jimmy Flynn**, born in Boston in 1934, is the Teamster Union official and actor who was sensationally tried and acquitted of murder in 1986.

Films he has appeared in include *The Cider House Rules* and *Good Will Hunting*.

In the world of literature, **Nick Flynn**, born in 1960 near Boston, is the poet and writer whose work has appeared in prestigious publications that include The New Yorker and the Paris Review, while **Greg Flynn**, born in Perth, Western

Australia, is the writer whose first novel, *The Berlin Cross*, was published in 2005.

Born in 1970, **Catherine O'Flynn** is the British writer whose first novel, *What Was Lost*, was published in 2007.

In the world of politics, **Edmund Flynn**, born in 1847 and who died in 1927, was the Canadian lawyer and member of the Conservative Party who was Premier of Quebec from 1896 to 1897.

Born in Providence, Rhode Island, in 1885, **William S. Flynn** was Governor of Rhode Island from 1923 until 1925, while **Raymond Flynn**, born in Hyde Park, Massachusetts, in 1939, is the former All-American basketball player who served as Democratic Mayor of Boston from 1984 to 1993 and as Ambassador to the Vatican from 1993 to 1997.

Born in 1939 in Castlebar, Co. Mayo, **Pádraig Flynn** is the former Irish politician who held a number of prominent government posts before his retirement, while **Patrick Flynn**, born in 1921 in Rathcormac, Co. Cork and who later immigrated with his family to Canada, was the Liberal Party politician who was Member of Parliament for Kitchener, Ontario, from 1974 until 1979.

In the highly competitive world of sport, **Patrick Flynn**, born in 1895, was the American athlete who took the silver medal in the steeplechase at the 1920 Olympics in Antwerp, while **Mike Flynn**, born in 1974 in Doylestown, Pennsylvania is, at the time of writing, a National Football League centre for the Baltimore Ravens.

In the creative world of music, **Liam O'Flynn**, born in 1945 in Kill, Co. Kildare, is the Irish folk musician also known as Liam Óg Ó Floinn.

A founder member of the band Planxty, he is also a session musician who has worked with a number of international artistes, including Kate Bush, Enya, and Mark Knopfler.

In a totally different musical genre **Robb Flynn**, born in 1968 in Oakland, California, is the guitarist and vocalist of the thrash metal band Machine Head, and a recipient of the rather impressive sounding Metal Hammer 2007 Golden God Award.

Moving to yet another sphere, **Harry Flynn**, born in 1933 in Schenectady, New York is, at the time of writing, the 7th Roman Catholic Archbishop and Ninth Bishop of the Archdiocese of Saint Paul and Minneapolis.

In the realms of law enforcement **William J. Flynn**, born in 1867 in New York City and who died in 1928, was a former head of America's Secret Service who is also credited with having reorganised New York's detective force.

In the world of science, **James R. Flynn**, born in Chicago in 1934, is the intelligence researcher now resident in New Zealand who is known for his discovery of what is known as the **Flynn Effect** – the continued year-on-year rise in IQ scores in all parts of the world.

It is also sometimes referred to as the Lynn-Flynn Effect,

in reference to the work of Richard Lynn who examined the role nutrition plays in intelligence.

Emeritus Professor of Political Studies at the University of Otago, in Dunedin, **James R. Flynn** is also a prominent campaigner for liberal causes.

Taking to the skies, the **Reverend John Flynn**, born in 1880 in Moliagul, Victoria, was the Australian Presbyterian minister who founded the country's Royal Flying Doctor Service – the world's first air ambulance.

Originally known as the Aerial Medical Service, it literally took off in 1928, operating from Cloncurry, in Queensland, thanks to Flynn's vision and determination.

In addition to establishing the flying doctor service, he also established a number of 'bush' hospitals in the vast Australian outback.

Awarded with the Order of the British Empire (O.B.E.) in 1933, Flynn died in 1951.

The Australian Electoral Commission named a newly created federal seat, Flynn, in his honour in 2006, while he is also featured on Australian currency.

Key dates in Ireland's history from the first settlers to the formation of the Irish Republic:

circa 7000 B.C.	Arrival and settlement of Stone Age people.
circa 3000 B.C.	Arrival of settlers of New Stone Age period.
circa 600 B.C.	First arrival of the Celts.
200 A.D.	Establishment of Hill of Tara, Co. Meath, as seat of the High Kings.
circa 432 A.D.	Christian mission of St. Patrick.
800-920 A.D.	Invasion and subsequent settlement of Vikings.
1002 A.D.	Brian Boru recognised as High King.
1014	Brian Boru killed at battle of Clontarf.
1169-1170	Cambro-Norman invasion of the island.
1171	Henry II claims Ireland for the English Crown.
1366	Statutes of Kilkenny ban marriage between native Irish and English.
1529-1536	England's Henry VIII embarks on religious Reformation.
1536	Earl of Kildare rebels against the Crown.
1541	Henry VIII declared King of Ireland.
1558	Accession to English throne of Elizabeth I.
1565	Battle of Affane.
1569-1573	First Desmond Rebellion.
1579-1583	Second Desmond Rebellion.
1594-1603	Nine Years War.
1606	Plantation' of Scottish and English settlers.

1607	Flight of the Earls.
1632-1636	Annals of the Four Masters compiled.
1641	Rebellion over policy of plantation and other grievances.
1649	Beginning of Cromwellian conquest.
1688	Flight into exile in France of Catholic Stuart monarch James II as Protestant Prince William of Orange invited to take throne of England along with his wife, Mary.
1689	William and Mary enthroned as joint monarchs; siege of Derry.
1690	Jacobite forces of James defeated by William at battle of the Boyne (July) and Dublin taken.
1691	Athlone taken by William; Jacobite defeats follow at Aughrim, Galway, and Limerick; conflict ends with Treaty of Limerick (October) and Irish officers allowed to leave for France.
1695	Penal laws introduced to restrict rights of Catholics; banishment of Catholic clergy.
1704	Laws introduced constricting rights of Catholics in landholding and public office.
1728	Franchise removed from Catholics.
1791	Foundation of United Irishmen republican movement.
1796	French invasion force lands in Bantry Bay.
1798	Defeat of Rising in Wexford and death of United Irishmen leaders Wolfe Tone and Lord Edward Fitzgerald.

1800	Act of Union between England and Ireland.
1803	Dublin Rising under Robert Emmet.
1829	Catholics allowed to sit in Parliament.
1845-1849	The Great Hunger: thousands starve to death as potato crop fails and thousands more emigrate.
1856	Phoenix Society founded.
1858	Irish Republican Brotherhood established.
1873	Foundation of Home Rule League.
1893	Foundation of Gaelic League.
1904	Foundation of Irish Reform Association.
1913	Dublin strikes and lockout.
1916	Easter Rising in Dublin and proclamation of an Irish Republic.
1917	Irish Parliament formed after Sinn Fein election victory.
1919-1921	War between Irish Republican Army and British Army.
1922	Irish Free State founded, while six northern counties remain part of United Kingdom as Northern Ireland, or Ulster; civil war up until 1923 between rival republican groups.
1949	Foundation of Irish Republic after all remaining constitutional links with Britain are severed.